S0-AJR-879

NEW ARCHAEOLOGICAL
FINDS IN CHINA

NEW ARCHAEOLOGICAL
FINDS IN CHINA

DISCOVERIES DURING THE CULTURAL REVOLUTION

FOREIGN LANGUAGES PRESS

PEKING   1974

First edition   1972
Second edition (revised)   1973
Second printing   1974

Publisher's Note

DURING the Great Proletarian Cultural Revolution, China's archaeological workers, guided by Chairman Mao's revolutionary line and supported by the broad worker, peasant and soldier masses, have done a great deal of work in preserving and excavating cultural objects. Their discoveries date from 2,000 years B.C. to the Ming Dynasty in the 17th century. Among the finds are many new or rare items important in the study of the political, economic, cultural and military aspects of different dynasties in Chinese history and the friendly intercourse between China and other lands.

This collection of articles deals with some of the important discoveries and cultural objects unearthed so far in the Cultural Revolution.

Printed in the People's Republic of China

Decorated red pottery tripod, late primitive society over 4,000 years ago. Unearthed in 1971 at Tsouhsien, Shantung.

Bronze owl wine jar (the cover was a later make), Shang Dynasty (1600-1028 B.C.). Unearthed in 1966 at Changsha, Hunan.

Ying yuan gol
coins, State of Ch'
(5th-3rd centurie
B.C.). Unearthe
in 1969 and 1970 a
Liuan and Funar
Anhwei.

Bronze ewer with loop handle, Shang Dynasty.
Unearthed in 1970 at Ninghsiang, Hunan.

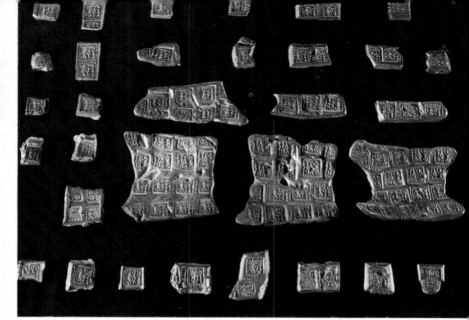

Pottery figurines of musicians, dancers and acrobats, Western Han Dynasty (206 B.C.-A.D. 24). Unearthed in 1969 at Tsinan, Shantung.

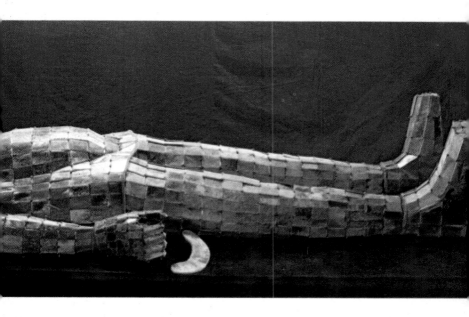

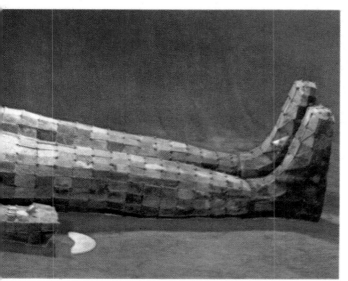

Jade clothes sewn with gold thread — burial clothes of Liu Sheng, Prince of Chungshan (*upper*) and his wife Tou Wan, middle of Western Han Dynasty (end of 2nd century B.C.). Unearthed in 1968 at Mancheng, Hopei.

Gilded bronze figurine with lamp, middle of Western
Han Dynasty. Unearthed in 1968 at Mancheng, Hopei.

Poshan incense burner inlaid with gold decorations, middle of Western Han Dynasty. Unearthed in 1968 at Mancheng, Hopei.

Two of the 40 bronze coins from Tou Wan's tomb.

Golden brown glazed porcelain flask, Northern Chi Dynasty (A.D. 550-577). Unearthed in 1971 at Anyang, Honan.

Gilded bronze ink-slab box, middle of Eastern Han Dynasty (about A.D. 117-145). Unearthed in 1969 at Hsuchow, Kiangsu.

Gold bowl with flower pattern, Tang Dynasty (A.D. 618-907). Unearthed in 1970 at Sian, Shensi.

Gilded silver wine pot with dancing horse clenching a cup in its teeth, Tang Dynasty during the mid-8th century. Unearthed in 1970 in Shensi.

Onyx rhyton (drinking horn) with ox snout in gold (from central Asia), Tang Dynasty during the mid-8th century. Unearthed at Sian, Shensi.

Black horse with three-colour decoration, Tang Dynasty. Unearthed in 1971 at Loyang, Honan.

Silk damask with flower
and bird pattern, Tang
Dynasty. Unearthed in
1966 at Turfan, Sinkiang.

Silk damask shoes with
cloud pattern toe, Tang
Dynasty. Unearthed in
1966 at Turfan, Sinkiang.

Blue and white flask with flying phoenix pattern, Yuan
Dynasty (1271-1368).   Unearthed in 1970 at Peking.

Contents

Archaeological Work During the
Cultural Revolution
Hsia Nai   1

Han Tombs at Mancheng
Ku Yen-wen   14

Tatu, the Yuan Capital
Ku Yen-wen   21

Finds from Kansu
Lan Hsin-wen   31

Ch'u Tomb and Weapons from
Changsha
Hsiang Po   35

Perfect Preservation After 2,100 Years
Chung Chien   42

More Finds Along the Silk Road
Hsia Nai   53

Tomb of the Ming Prince of Lu
Lu Wen-kao   61

The Masses Support Archaeological
Work
Chang Li-chuan and Lin Yu-ching   66

*Hsia Nai**

Archaeological Work
During the Cultural Revolution

*D*URING the Great Proletarian Cultural Revolution, China's archaeological workers took an active part in the revolutionary struggle and at the same time did much work in their field. They did not work in isolation but among the people, following the mass line. Workers, peasants or soldiers report ancient relics as soon as they find them and co-operate fully with the archaeological teams which follow up on these leads. This has made the archaeological work develop smoothly and yield richer results than ever before both in new finds in old sites and in the discovery of previously unknown sites.

New Discoveries of Pre-Han Period

New finds in famous archaeological sites are numerous, some of them startling. In 1967 more skull fragments of

---

*Hsia Nai is Director of the Institute of Archaeology, Chinese Academy of Sciences.

1

Peking Man (*Sinanthropus pekinensis*) and stone implements were unearthed at Choukoutien,[1] southwest of Peking. This 500,000 years old primitive man was one of the ancestors of China's present nationalities.

In 1968 and 1971, more bronze, jade and earthenware pieces were found in cemeteries of the Yin Dynasty[2] (latter half of second millennium B.C.) at Anyang, Honan Province.

Bronze vessels of the Western Chou Dynasty[3] (about 1027-771 B.C.) were unearthed in 1966 and 1967 at Chishan County near Sian, Shensi Province, and between 1964 and 1970 at Peiyaotsun in suburban Loyang, Honan. The former includes some vessels bearing inscriptions. Over 400 tombs of the Western Chou Dynasty have been discovered at the latter site. Though most of them had been robbed before liberation, jade, bronze weapons, a few bronze ritual vessels and vessels of proto-porcelain were found.

The tombs of the State of Ch'u[4] at Changsha, Hunan Province, have long been known throughout the world. In 1971 a relatively early tomb was opened at Liuchengchiao, Changsha, perhaps dating from the early Warring States Period[5] (about 5th century B.C.). The well-preserved articles in the tomb include a 23-stringed zither,[6] a bronze *chi*[7] halberd, a bronze *ko*[8] dagger-axe and a bronze *mao*[9] spear, all with lacquered wooden shafts intact (lengths: 3.03 m., 1.4 m. and 2.8 m. respectively), lacquerware, silk cloth and other items.

Between 1969 and 1970 continued excavation of sacrificial pits at the site of the State of Tsin[10] at Houma,

Shansi Province, yielded the bones of sacrificial oxen, horses and sheep, jade blades and slips, and other relics from the 5th century B.C. In 1969 several tombs from the middle and end of the Warring States Period (403-221 B.C.) containing sacrificed slaves were dug up in the same area.

New Finds Along the Silk Road

Between 1966 and 1969, 114 tombs dating from the 5th to the 7th centuries were excavated in the famous Astana and Karakhoja cemeteries at Turfan in Sinkiang. The objects of greatest interest were the well-preserved silks, including silk damask and polychrome silk with designs executed by coating the parts not to be dyed with wax (batik), or by knotting the silk in skeins. There were documents written in Han characters, such as contracts and name lists.

Treasures of Hochiatsun, Sian

The most exciting finds were at Sian and Loyang, capitals of the Tang Dynasty (A.D. 618-907). In 1970 a hoard consisting of two pottery jugs was found at Hochiatsun, a southern suburb of Sian. The jugs contained over 1,000 items, including gold and silver vessels, jade objects, precious stones, jewelry, medicinal minerals (cinnabar, stalactite, amethyst, litharge, etc.), and Chinese and foreign coins.

The gold and silver vessels alone accounted for over 200 items, an unprecedentedly important find from the Tang Dynasty. Beautifully shaped, they include six-lobed bowls, lotus-shaped bowls, stem cups, two octagonal cups with handles, peach-shaped dishes, ewers with loop handles, winged cups and incense burners. Many of the objects have delicate and beautiful designs made by casting, repoussé, tracing, filigree, granulation and openwork. In order to bring out the design, the casting or repoussé decorations usually have a ring-matted background, and the designs of the silver vessels are often gilded. Decorative patterns include floral sprays and scrolls, acanthus, animal motifs (lion, fox, horse, bear, phoenix, parrot, mandarin duck, a pair of fish, tortoise, etc.) and hunting scenes popular in the Tang Dynasty. Each face of the octagonal gold cups has musicians and dancers in high relief. The objects show the creative wisdom and skill of the working people of ancient times.

The gold and silver vessels of Sassanian Persia obviously influenced the shape and design of many pieces, but the Tang gold and silver smiths assimilated this essence and sinicized it. The hoard includes some foreign objects such as a glass bowl with circle decor, an onyx rhyton (drinking horn) with the ox's snout in gold, a Sassanian silver coin (Chosroes II, A.D. 590-627), a Byzantine gold coin (Heraclius, A.D. 610-641), and five Japanese silver coins (*Wadokaiho*, minted in A.D. 708). This strengthens evidence that communications between China and other countries were well developed at the time.

The hoard was found at the site of the mansion of the Prince of Pin,[11] Li Shou-li[12] (died in A.D. 741), cousin of the emperor Hsuan Tsung.[13] The mansion continued to be used by his son, the next Prince of Pin. Silver discs in the find are inscribed with dates such as "19th year of K'ai Yuan[14]" (A.D. 731). Possibly a member of the family of the new Prince of Pin buried the hoard before fleeing to Szechuan with the emperor Hsuan Tsung, his family and high officials of the court when a subordinate of An Lu-shan attacked Changan in the 15th year of T'ien Pao[15] (A.D. 756). The person who buried the hoard supposedly died unexpectedly, and no one else knew where it was.

Hanchia State Granary

Between 1969 and 1971 the remains of the Hanchia state granary[16] of the Tang Dynasty were discovered and unearthed at Loyang, its eastern capital. No works of art were discovered, but the new finds are important in the study of economic history. Like the discoveries at Sian, they reveal the cruel exploitation the working people suffered under the Tang ruling class.

The building of the Hanchia granary was started in the first year of the reign of Ta Yeh[17] (A.D. 605) during the Sui Dynasty.[18] It was located northeast of the Loyang palace and was one of the main state granaries of the Tang

5

Dynasty. A wall encircled an area of 420,000 square metres, enclosing about 400 round storehouses ranged in symmetrical rows. Of varying size, from 6 to 18 metres in diameter and 5 to 10 metres in depth, they were apparently subterranean or semi-subterranean.

The roof structure could not be ascertained. But signs that wooden boards had been used for lining the walls were apparent. The lower part was constructed to provide ventilation. Half a metre above the ground a row of thin timber sleepers ran from one side of the wall to the other. Wooden boards were placed on top of these. This provided air circulation which kept the space above fairly dry and prevented the grain from becoming damp and mildewed.

Every storehouse had bricks with inscriptions carved on them specifying its position in the granary, the quantity of grain stored, the year and month it was stored and the status and name of the storekeeper. The bricks discovered so far mainly date about the end of the 7th century (A.D. 692-699). The grain came from many places, including Soochow and Yenchow (now Chienteh County in Chekiang Province) in the south and Hsingchow (now Hsingtai County in Hopei Province) and Chichow in the north. A large storehouse held over 10,000 *tan*[19] (1 *tan* of the Tang period is equal to about 60 litres). In some, decayed millet was discovered. The storekeepers were of many different statuses, showing that the granary was managed through a strict administrative system.

The Tang ruling class exploited the peasants by a cruel system of land taxation. Grain was brought to the capital from many parts of the country and even a canal was built for this purpose. The rulers used the grain extorted from the working people to pay the very officials and army who suppressed and enslaved them. The state granaries played the role of the state bank or national treasury in present capitalist countries.

Tatu, Capital of Yuan Dynasty

The site of the Yuan Dynasty[20] (A.D. 1271-1368) capital Tatu[21] was surveyed and partly unearthed in Peking between 1965 and 1969. The city plan of the northeastern part of the capital (now in the eastern part of the northern suburb) has been ascertained. The basic lay-out was a gridiron pattern of main streets running north-south and east-west, dividing the area into rectangular blocks. Corbelled watergates for drainage made of stone blocks were unearthed under the capital's east and west city walls. Strips of pig-iron were dovetailed between the blocks to join and strengthen them.

In 1969, at the western wall of the barbican (the outer defensive work of the gateway) of the later Hsi Chih Men Gate,[22] remnants of the Yuan Dynasty Ho Yi Men Gate[23] were uncovered. This had been walled up with bricks during the early part of the Ming Dynasty[24] (15th century). Part of the gate-tower walls, over a metre high, still remained.

On these and the walls of the entrance were graffiti with the reigning names of the Yuan Dynasty, one of them dated 1358. The Yuan Dynasty city walls were built of rammed earth. The vaulted outer gateway of Ho Yi Men was built with fired bricks smaller than the bricks of the Ming Dynasty. The excavations gave us a vivid picture of the sweeping grandeur of this Yuan Dynasty capital. No wonder Marco Polo had endless praise for this great city, which he called "Taidu" or "Cambaluc" (Khanbaligh), when he visited it (1271-1295) during his trip to China.

In the beginning of the Ming Dynasty (1368-1644) the northern wall of the city was moved southward. It thus covered up the remains of many Yuan Dynasty houses. Between 1965 and 1969 archaeologists excavated several such sites which had remained comparatively intact. Large mansions were laid out in the shape of ⊥, a roofed passage connecting the front rooms with the back chambers. Many polychrome glazed pottery and terra-cotta architectural decorations were discovered, as well as articles of daily use made of pottery, porcelain and other materials. The remnants of the cover of a lacquer case showed a beautifully delicate design, inlaid with mother-of-pearl, of Kuang Han Kung, the Moon Palace.[25]

Han Tombs at Mancheng

Finds in the last few years were not limited to known archaeological sites. Important discoveries have also been made in many new or not well-known places.

One of these is the opening of two Han Dynasty tombs west of Mancheng,[26] Hopei Province, in 1968. The tombs were cut deep into the cliffs of rocky Lingshan Mountain. In the central chamber and two side chambers of each tomb, there had originally been wooden structures with tiled roofs. These had decayed and collapsed. Inside were placed a large number of pottery vessels, carts and horses together with their ornaments, and other funeral objects. In the rear chamber was a small structure of stone slabs housing the coffin and the most precious of the funeral furniture.

Over 2,800 objects were unearthed from the two tombs. Among these are bronze vessels of especially high technical and artistic level, including a pair of bronze hu[27] vessels inlaid with gold and silver bird script, an inlaid gilded bronze hu vessel, a bronze hu vessel and a Poshan incense burner[28] inlaid with gold, a gilded figure with a lamp, and bronze lamps in the shape of a lamb or a bird.

There were fragments of very fine silk in plain weave (200 warp and 90 weft threads per square centimetre), embroidery and silk damask. Other new finds were dozens of gold discs and gold ornaments with patterns in repoussé.

The two dead were enveloped in jade cases, something like ancient Egyptian mummy cases. These were called "jade clothes sewn with gold thread"[29] and covered the whole body. One was made of 2,690 and the other of 2,156 small rectangular pieces of jade with holes at the four corners, tied together with fine gold thread. Such cases, given them by the emperor in the Han Dynasty, were only worn by high-ranking nobility after death. This is the first find of such complete jade cases.

The two dead held jade crescents in their hands and each had a jade pillow with a gold dragon head at each end. Many of the bronzes buried with them had inscriptions recording the name of the palatial residence, name of the object, the date and the amount of bronze used, etc. According to these inscriptions and the jade cases worn by the dead, the tombs are those of the well-known Liu Sheng,[30] Prince Ching of Chungshan[31] (who died in the 4th year of Yuan Ting,[32] or 113 B.C.), and his wife; they lived in the middle of the Western Han Dynasty.[33]

This discovery was a penetrating exposure of the idle and extravagant life of the feudal ruling class based on their cruel oppression and exploitation of the working people.

Some Other Discoveries

Western Han Dynasty tombs were also excavated at Tsinan, Shantung Province, in 1969. A set of pottery figurines of acrobats and musicians and a pair of pottery birds with *hu* vessels and tripod *ting*[34] vessels on their wings reveal shapes never seen before.

An Eastern Han Dynasty[35] tomb with stone reliefs dating from the first year of Yung Ch'u[36] (A.D. 107) was discovered in 1969 at Michih, northern Shensi Province. This provided new material from an area where Han Dynasty stone reliefs had only been found after liberation.

In 1965 and 1966, the tomb of Ssuma Chin-lung[37] (who died in A.D. 484), a high official of the Northern Wei Dynasty,[38] was excavated at Tatung, Shansi Province. In this tomb were found wooden screens with lacquer paintings, two pairs of sculptured stone pillar-bases, a coffin platform decorated with reliefs, several porcelain vessels, and a great number of funeral figurines of pottery, both glazed and unglazed.

In 1971 the tomb of Fan Tsui,[39] governor of Liangchow, who died in A.D. 575 in the Northern Chi Dynasty,[40] was opened at Anyang, Honan Province. A great number of pottery figurines, several early celadons and a pair of brown glazed flat flasks with imprints of dancers and musicians were found.

At Wuwei County, Anhwei Province, a monk's tomb of the third year of Ching Yu[41] (1036) of the Northern Sung Dynasty[42] was discovered. A glass bottle, printed copies of the Buddhist *Dharani* sutras and dated documents were found.

In 1970 at Tsouhsien County, Shantung Province, the tomb of Chu Tan[43] (1370-1389), Prince of Lu,[44] was unearthed. At Chengtu, Szechuan Province, the tomb of Chu Yueh-lien[45] (1388-1409), eldest son of the Prince of Shu,[46] was unearthed. Both tombs belong to the imperial family of early Ming Dynasty.

The latter tomb had been robbed. Nevertheless, tricolour glazed pottery figurines found resemble, in shape, those of the wooden figurines found in the former tomb.

The tomb in Shantung was intact with many objects well preserved. In the front chamber more than 400 wooden figurines of various kinds were discovered. In the back chamber the prince's headdresses, robes, writing-brushes, an ink-stick, paper and an ink-stone were found. There were also a 7-stringed zither, black and white pieces and a paper board for the chess game of *wei ch'i*,[47] several sheets of calligraphy from the Yuan Dynasty, four paintings and 22 books of the same dynasty, and many pieces of model furniture made of bamboo, wood or metal.

Serving Proletarian Politics

Discoveries made during the Great Proletarian Cultural Revolution reveal more facts in the historical process of mankind creating the world, the working people creating social wealth. The new finds extend from a half million years ago to the 17th century. Under the rule of the feudal dynasties, it was the imperial family and the nobility, not the working people, who enjoyed the material wealth. History written during the feudal dynasties naturally reversed the truth that it is the masses of the people who create history.

Ancient cultural objects unearthed today provide valuable material in the study of the politics, economics and culture of the primitive, slave and feudal societies of China.

Tempered in the Cultural Revolution and advancing along the revolutionary path pointed out by Chairman Mao, Chinese archaeologists are contributing much evidence for the scientific materialist view of history.

[1]周口店. [2]殷. [3]西周. [4]楚. [5]战国. [6]瑟. [7]戟. [8]戈. [9]矛. [10]晋国. [11]邬王. [12]李守礼. [13]玄宗. [14]开元. [15]天宝. [16]含嘉仓. [17]大业. [18]隋. [19]石. [20]元. [21]大都. [22]西直门. [23]和义门. [24]明. [25]"广寒宫". [26]满城. [27]壶. [28]博山炉. [29]"金缕玉衣". [30]刘胜. [31]中山靖王. [32]元鼎. [33]西汉. [34]鼎. [35]东汉. [36]永初. [37]司马金龙. [38]北魏. [39]范粹. [40]北齐. [41]景祐. [42]北宋. [43]朱檀. [44]鲁. [45]朱悦燫. [46]蜀. [47]围棋.

Ku Yen-wen

Han Tombs at Mancheng

*T*WO spacious Han tombs were discovered in Lingshan Mountain in the western suburb of Mancheng, Hopei Province, in 1968. The excavation took two months, from July to September.

This archaeological work was done with the deep concern of the Central Committee of the Communist Party headed by Chairman Mao. The officers and men of the Chinese People's Liberation Army were the first to discover one of the tombs. With the close co-operation between the Institute of Archaeology of the Chinese Academy of Sciences and the Archaeological Team of Hopei Province and thanks to vigorous support and assistance from the P.L.A. and the local revolutionary masses, this tomb was excavated.

Lingshan is a mountain ranging north-south, about 200 metres high. Its rocky surface is bare except for scattered clusters of weeds. The area above the tomb is littered with rock chips obviously left from building the tomb. Rock chips were also found about 100 metres to the north of this tomb, indicating another tomb in the vicinity. Hence the discovery of the second tomb.

The first tomb was that of Liu Sheng, Prince Ching of Chungshan of the Western Han Dynasty (206 B.C.-A.D.24), and the second that of his wife Tou Wan.[1] The tombs, cut deep into the rocky cliffs, are literally underground palaces, whose magnitude bespeaks a building project herculean for that time. Liu Sheng's tomb is 52 metres long, 37 metres wide and about 7 metres high, occupying a space of 2,700 cubic metres. Tou Wan's tomb is the larger by 300 cubic metres. It is estimated that the opening of such enormous cliff-tombs would require the labour of several

Liu Sheng's tomb, inside.

hundred men with modern technique for a whole year. The manpower and material resources involved in the construction over 2,000 years ago are scarcely imaginable.

The two tombs are similar in shape and

Tou Wan's tomb, main chamber.

structure. Each tomb is divided into a central chamber, two auxiliary chambers on the southern and northern sides, and a rear chamber. In front of the central chamber, whose door faces east, is a long underground passage. In each of the central and auxiliary chambers had been a wooden tiled-roof structure which had already collapsed, while in the rear chamber was a stone-slab structure with slanting roof.

In Liu Sheng's tomb the south chamber enclosed several chariots and about a dozen horses and in the north chamber were stored several hundred pieces of earthenware of various kinds for holding foodstuffs and wine. The central chamber was a grand hall in which a variety of bronze vessels, lacquerware and earthenware, as well as many pottery and stone figurines, were placed in an orderly way. The rear chamber was the inner room housing the coffin and the most precious of the furniture and vessels, and attached to it was a room for bathing. Tou Wan's tomb and its contents followed roughly the same pattern.

The underground passages were blocked with stones and earth after the burial, and the doors at the ends of the passages sealed by pouring molten iron between two parallel brick walls to make a wall of iron.

Over 2,800 funeral objects were discovered in the two tombs, including bronze vessels, gold, silver, iron, glass and jade articles, earthenware, lacquerware and silk fabrics. Many are of high technical and artistic level, and some are of types never discovered before. They provide important material for studying the development of metallurgy, sculpture, weaving and other arts and crafts 2,000 years ago.

Delicate and beautiful in design, the bronze vessels are artistically made by tracing and repoussé. A Poshan incense burner, for instance, used by Han Dynasty nobles, is inlaid with gold in all-over pattern. Its lid is shaped like a mountain with undulating peaks, in which hunters pursue wild animals. It is far more elegant and refined than most Poshan incense burners so far discovered. A pair of bronze *chung*[2] wine containers covered with a bird script (an ancient form of seal character) and other designs inlaid with gold and silver are among the finest extant. Two gilded bronze wine containers, one with a coiled-dragon design and the other with a knob design, are intricate in decoration and rich in colour; their lustre remains after 2,000 years underground. There is a bronze "scarlet bird" lamp, with a flying bird holding in its beak a round tripartite dish which contains three candlesticks. Still more attractive is the *Ch'ang Hsin* Lamp[3] from Tou Wan's tomb, named from the two characters meaning eternal fidelity inscribed inside. Beautifully and skilfully designed, the lamp takes the shape of a palace serving girl, who holds the lamp. The lamp is movable and the lampshade adjustable so that the direction and intensity of the light can be controlled. The girl's head is detachable, and the body is hollow, her right arm being a pipe through which the smoke is directed into the body, keeping the room free of smoke.

The two bodies of Liu Sheng and Tou Wan were enveloped in "jade clothes sewn with gold thread." The first complete jade burial clothes ever discovered, they were well preserved and have been restored to their original form. The jade clothes, also known as jade cases, were reserved exclusively for Han emperors and high-ranking aristocrats. According to the feudal hierarchy, jade clothes were sewn with gold, silver or bronze thread according to grade. The jade was cut into small, thin rectangular or square wafers, which were joined with gold thread through tiny holes in the four corners of each piece. Liu Sheng's clothes are made up of 2,690 pieces of jade sewn with 1,110 grammes of gold thread, that of Tou Wan composed of 2,156 pieces of jade sewn with 703 grammes of gold thread. The two jade suits indicate the early artisans' high technical skill. Marks left on the jade show that it was cut with a delicate saw with 0.3 mm. teeth. Holes at the corners were one mm. in diameter, bored with a tube-type drill (sand drilling). First-class workmanship is also shown in the making of the gold thread. Some was made of 12 fine gold strands, pliable and strong. Judging from present-day handicrafts, it would have taken an expert jade-smith of the Han Dynasty more than 10 years to complete such a suit.

The great leader Chairman Mao has pointed out: **"In China education has always been the exclusive preserve of the landlords, and the peasants have had no access to it. But the landlords' culture is created by the peasants, for its sole source is the peasants' sweat and blood."** Every cultural find from the Han tombs bears the sweat and blood of the working people. For instance, the inscriptions on two bronze water jugs from Tou Wan's tomb say they were bought from Hotung (present-day Hsiahsien County, Shansi Province), the price mark on one being 840 cash. *Han Shu*[4] (*History of the Han Dynasty*) says that apart from the land rent adults from ages 15 to 56 paid 120 cash a year as poll-tax, and children from ages 3 to 14 paid 23 cash a year. This imposed such a heavy burden on impoverished peasants that poor people "kill their own children as soon as they are born." The cost of one plain bronze jug (840 cash) was twice the annual poll-tax for a 5-member household (two adults and three children).

Liu Sheng, elder brother of the emperor Wu Ti of Han,[5] was notorious for his depravity and corruption, precisely as Ssuma Chien,[6] great historian and man of letters, wrote in his *Shih Chi*[7] (*Historical Records*): "Liu Sheng is fond of wine and women." He and his wife levied exorbitant taxes on the 600,000 people in his fief, the Principality of Chungshan, embracing 14 counties. They forced thousands of working people to build these two "underground palaces" for them and ordered large quantities of priceless objects to be buried with them in their tombs. The archaeological work has mercilessly exposed their evils and extravagance as well as their brutal exploitation and oppression of the working people.

Like many other important archaeological undertakings in China, the excavation of the Han tombs at Mancheng not only aids the study of ancient Chinese society but also provides vivid data for popular education in ideology, politics and class struggle.

---

[1]窦绾. [2]钟. [3]"长信宫灯". [4]《汉书》. [5]汉武帝. [6]司马迁. [7]《史记》.

Ku Yen-wen

Tatu, the Yuan Capital

*P*EKING is a city with a long history. The rulers of the Liao Dynasty[1] (A.D. 916-1125) were the first to establish their capital here and called it "Nanching" (Southern Capital). The Kin Dynasty[2] (1115-1234) rulers also made it their capital and named it "Chungtu" (Middle Capital). In the Yuan Dynasty (1271-1368), a new capital was built northeast of the old, Liao-Kin Dynasty capital, and this was named Tatu[3] (Great Capital).

The building of Tatu began in the 4th year of the reign of Chih Yuan[4] (1267). Grand in scale and systematic in plan, it was a metropolis of contemporary world fame. After the Yuan Dynasty, the Ming rulers gradually rebuilt and expanded the southern half of Tatu into the Peking (Northern Capital) of the Ming and, following that, the Ching Dynasty.[5]

The archaeological work of Tatu has been carried out jointly by the Institute of Archaeology of the Chinese Academy of Sciences and the Peking Municipal Archaeological Bureau. After several years of investigations and surveying of its city walls, streets, rivers and lakes, the foundations of a dozen various types of buildings were excavated. Particularly since 1969, in conjunction with building construction, large-scale excavation work has been done at the barbican entrance to Ho Yi Men[6] (Gate of Harmony and Righteousness) and at a number of dwelling sites behind Yung Ho Kung[7] (Harmony and Peace Lamasery). This work has cast a great deal of light on the class struggle, social life and town planning of the Yuan Dynasty. It also provides useful materials for rapid construction in our capital.

Extensive investigations and excavations at key points have revealed the structure and outline of the Tatu outer walls. The walls, built of rammed earth, were as thick as 24 metres at the base. The city was rectangular in shape, a little longer from north to south. The circumference was 28,600 metres. Tatu's southern wall was south of the present East and West Ch'angan Boulevard,[8] while the southern sections of the eastern and western walls coincided with those of Peking in the Ming and Ching periods. Remnants of the northern wall and the northern section of the eastern and western walls still remain visible today at "Earth City"[9] in the northern suburb of Peking.

There were altogether 11 city gates, the three in the eastern wall being: Kuang Hsi Men[10] (Bright and Splendid Gate), east of the present Ho P'ing Li;[11] Ch'ung Jen Men[12] (Gate of Upholding Benevolence), later Tung Chih Men;[13] and Ch'i Hua Men[14] (Gate of Uniformity and Affinity), later Ch'ao Yang Men.[15] The three gates in the southern wall were Wen Ming Men[16] (Gate of Culture and Brightness), now Tung Tan;[17] Li Cheng Men[18] (Gate of Beauty and Uprightness), now south of Tien An Men,[19] and Shun Ch'eng Men[20] (Gate of Modest Deference), now Hsi Tan.[21]

Sketch Map of Yuan's Tatu Compared with Peking of Ming and Ching

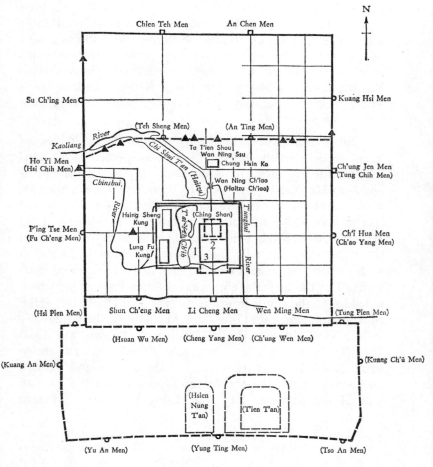

N

Chien Teh Men   An Chen Men

Su Ch'ing Men   Kuang Hsi Men

Kaoliang   River   (Teh Sheng Men)   (An Ting Men)

Ho Yi Men
(Hsi Chih Men)   Chi Shui T'an (Haitzu)   Ta T'ien Shou
Wan Ning Ssu
Chung Hsin Ko   Ch'ung Jen Men
(Tung Chih Men)

Chinshui   Wan Ning Ch'iao
(Haitzu Ch'iao)

River   Hsing Sheng
Kung   T'a-yeh Ch'ih   (Ching Shan)   Tungchi
River

P'ing Tse Men
(Fu Ch'eng Men)   Lung Fu
Kung   1   2
3   Ch'i Hua Men
(Ch'ao Yang Men)

(Hsi Pien Men)   Shun Ch'eng Men   Li Cheng Men   Wen Ming Men   (Tung Pien Men)

(Hsuan Wu Men)   (Cheng Yang Men)   (Ch'ung Wen Men)

(Kuang An Men)   (Kuang Ch'ü Men)

(Hsien
Nung
T'an)   (T'ien T'an)

(Yu An Men)   (Yung Ting Men)   (Tso An Men)

Legend

1 Imperial City (Yuan)

2 Palace City (Yuan)

3 Imperial Palaces
(Ming and Ching)

▲ ·········· Excavation site

——— ······· Tatu of Yuan

⌒ ······ River or lake of Tatu

– – – ······· Peking of Ming and
Ching Periods

The three gates in the western wall were P'ing Tse Men[22] (Gate of Just Rule), later Fu Ch'eng Men;[23] Ho Yi Men (Gate of Harmony and Righteousness), later Hsi Chih Men;[24] and Su Ch'ing Men[25] (Gate of Respect and Purity), west of the present Peking Teachers' University. The two gates in the northern wall were Chien Teh Men[26] (Gate of High Virtue), now Teh Sheng Men Hsiao Kuan,[27] and An Chen Men[28] (Gate of Serenity and Chastity), now An Ting Men Hsiao Kuan.[29]*

Investigations of the Imperial and Palace Cities of Yuan reveal that the Imperial City was located in the centre of southern Tatu. Its eastern wall lay west of the present Nan Ho Yen[30] and Pei Ho Yen,[31] while its western wall was at the present western Huang Ch'eng Ken,[32] and its northern wall was south of the later Ti An Men.[33] Ling Hsing Men[34] (Bright Star Gate) at mid-point of the Yuan southern wall, was near the present Wu Men[35] (Meridian Gate) of the Ming and Ching Imperial Palaces. The eastern half of the Imperial City was the Yuan Palace City which extended in the south from the present T'ai Ho Tien[36] (Hall of Supreme Harmony) in Palace Museum to the Children's Palace in Chingshan Park[37] (formerly known as "Coal Hill"[38]) in the north. The eastern and western enclosures of the Palace City were near the eastern and western enclosures of the present Palace Museum. In the western half of the Imperial City were Lung Fu Kung[39] (Palace

---

*Since liberation, Peking's city planning has made necessary the removal of the old city walls and gates. Today, with the exception of a few gate towers, the walls and gates have been pulled down to make way for thoroughfares.

24

of Eminent Blessing), Hsing Sheng Kung[40] (Palace of Rising Sages) and T'ai Yeh Ch'ih[41] (Pond of Heavenly Dew).

The north-south axis of Tatu city ran from Li Cheng Men in the south, crossed the Yuan Imperial and Palace Cities, passed Wan Ning Ch'iao[42] (Myriad Peace Bridge), now Ti An Men Bridge, and ended at Chung Hsin Ko[43] (Central Pavilion) of Ta T'ien Shou Wan Ning Ssu[44] (Great Heavenly Longevity and Myriad Peace Temple), now Bell Tower.[45] This was also the axis of Peking during the Ming and Ching periods. Excavations have revealed traces of a section of a north-south road north of Chingshan, a section of the thoroughfare on the Tatu axis.

The streets of Tatu were well planned, according to the Italian Marco Polo who then sojourned in China. Praising Tatu's beautiful and perfect town planning, he wrote: "The lines are marked out uniformly and systematically ... like a chessboard." Investigations have shown that the lay-out of Tatu's streets featured many *hutung* (lanes), equidistant from one another, branching from and perpendicular to the north-south thoroughfares. Not a few streets and *hutung* in Peking today still bear traces of the street patterns of the Yuan Dynasty.

Water, always a vital question in town planning, was supplied to Tatu from two sources. One was the waterway of the Kaoliang[46] and T'unghui rivers,[47] and Haitzu Lake,[48] over which tribute rice was sent to the city. The other was the system formed by the Chinshui River[49] and T'ai Yeh Ch'ih, which supplied water to the palaces. Excavations have revealed the water gate through which the Chinshui River entered the city, its course within the city, and also its condition during the Ming Dynasty when the river silted up and gradually dried up at places. The extent and direction of other rivers and lakes have also been determined.

Two stone drainage culverts were discovered under the foundations of the rammed earth walls along the middle section of Tatu's eastern city wall and the northern section of its western city wall. These culverts had been built before the rammed-earth city walls were erected. The remains of their bases still show their structure. In 1970 near the present Hsi Ssu,[50] an open drainage channel was discovered west of Tatu's north-south thoroughfare. One metre wide and 1.65 metres deep, it was built with stone slabs and covered at crossroads. On a stone wall of the channel is an inscription carved by a contemporary stonemason: "Stonemason Liu San,[51] fifth moon, the 1st year of the reign of Chih Ho[52]" (A.D. 1328).

Chairman Mao has pointed out: **"The peasants and the handicraft workers were the basic classes which created the wealth and culture of this society."** Liu San was one of the great number of craftsmen who built the Tatu city. They were conscripted from different parts of the country, forced to do unpaid labour. No one knows how many died there after untold suffering. Every brick, every stone in the ancient city was laved with the blood and sweat of the working people.

The acute class antagonism in Yuan society is reflected in the ruins of some residences recently discovered. Excavation of two fairly complete courtyards behind Yung Ho Kung and Hou Ying Fang[53] sharply exposed the idle and extravagant life of the feudal ruling class. The common

26

characteristics of these two places were: the sites were high and dry; the main buildings were built on brick foundations; the lower part of the walls of some buildings (such as those at Hou Ying Fang) were built by "smoothened bricks with regular bonding"; the flooring was of square bricks, and there were elegantly patterned latticed doors. A lacquerware piece unearthed behind Yung Ho Kung was inscribed, "For use in the inner mansion." A black and white porcelain vase unearthed at Hou Ying Fang was also inscribed with the words "inner mansion." These objects indicate a close relationship between the owners and the feudal emperor. The central motif of a lacquer plate (fragment) unearthed at Hou Ying Fang is inlaid with mother-of-pearl and pictures Ch'ang Ngo[54] (a legendary beauty) escaping to the moon. The background is Kuang Han Kung (Palace of Cold Vastness in the Moon). The piece, a rare treasure of Yuan times, reflects the luxurious life of the feudal ruling class at the time. It also shows the level of accomplishment in lacquerware decorative art which the working people of ancient China had attained.

In 1970, upon opening the city wall at the old Drum Tower Street,[55] a cache of 16 porcelains was discovered among the ruins of a feudal ruling class residence. The cache was less than half a metre deep, and covered with a pottery basin. Among the porcelains are two *ying ch'ing* celadon bowls, each inscribed with brush and black ink with the Phatspa script.* These valuable porcelains were

---

*Phatspa script (八思巴字) was a Mongolian phonetic system which Kublai Khan ordered the linguist Phatspa to work out based on the Tibetan script. It was formally promulgated in the 6th year of Chih Yuan's reign (A.D. 1269) and used mainly in Yuan official documents.

obviously hastily stowed away by Yuan rulers facing their downfall and preparing to escape. It exposes the greediness of exploiting classes and their sinister scheme to make a comeback. Nine porcelains of blue and white (porcelains with blue pattern on white background), which include a phoenix-head flask and a small bowl with tray, are delightful in shape, fresh in colour and of high artistic value. The blue and white porcelains were a new product of the Yuan Dynasty, and an important landmark in the history of Chinese porcelain. Most of those previously discovered have belonged to the Ming period. The present group shows a high artistic level in the technique of shaping, glazing and decoration, and its discovery provides new reliable materials for studying the art of porcelain in the Yuan Dynasty.

The dwellings of the working people of the time were crude and poor. In the ruins of a tiny hut unearthed at the present Middle School No. 106 were only a stove, a *k'ang* (brick bed) and a stone mortar. The walls were of broken bricks, the floor was damp and 40 cm. lower than the doorway. The pottery utensils were cheap and

Site of Ho Yi Men of Yuan's Tatu and its gate tower.

28

crude. Life in such a hut contrasts drastically with the luxury of the large mansions of the feudal ruling class.

In the summer of 1969, the barbican entrance to Ho Yi Men of the Yuan period was discovered by workers dismantling the Arrow Tower at Hsi Chih Men. History records that in the 3rd moon of the 18th year of Chih Cheng[56] (1358) an insurgent peasant army attacked the suburbs of Tatu. The Yuan emperor Shun Ti[57] was panic-stricken. Preparing to flee, he ordered barbicans built for all 11 city gates and drawbridges thrown over the moats outside to strengthen Tatu's defences for a last-ditch struggle. These projects, done under pressure of the emergency, were completed in little more than a year.

An inscription on the grey walls above the barbican entrance to Ho Yi Men says that the structure was added in 1358. The remains of the gateway with its superstructure measure 22 metres high, the aperture being 10 metres long, 4.62 metres wide and 6.68 metres high. The two wooden doors and door frames were no more, but the stone blocks at both sides for installing the doors remained. There were three rooms in the gate tower like forts, with stairways on two sides. The structure of the gate indicates that it was hastily built, when the Yuan rulers were in a most precarious situation. The tall structure was built without foundations, and of inferior materials. However, they used a brick arch for the gateway, stronger than the wooden gateway of the lintel type which had been used since the Tang and Sung dynasties. On the floor of the gate tower were cisterns from which water could be let out over the wooden doors through five openings for defence against attacks by fire. These were new innovations in Chinese architecture.

The investigations and excavations at Tatu, like other archaeological work, have been done with the support and assistance of the workers, peasants and soldiers. The discovery of the barbican entrance to Ho Yi Men, in particular, should be attributed to the workers tearing down the Peking city walls. When this city gate was brought to light, they carefully protected the site and copied down the inscriptions written in ink when the gate was rebuilt in the 14th year of Hung Wu[58] in the Ming Dynasty (1381). (The inscriptions rapidly became illegible after being exposed to the air.) They also provided all possible conditions to help the archaeological workers in excavations. This is a manifestation of the worker, peasant and soldier masses' deeper love for the splendid cultural heritage of the motherland after conscientious study, during the Cultural Revolution, of Chairman Mao's teaching, **make the past serve the present.**

[1]辽．　[2]金．　[3]大都．　[4]至元．　[5]清．　[6]和义门．　[7]雍和宫．　[8]东西长安街．　[9]"土城"．　[10]光熙门．　[11]和平里．　[12]崇仁门．　[13]东直门．　[14]齐化门．　[15]朝阳门．　[16]文明门．　[17]东单．　[18]丽正门．　[19]天安门．　[20]顺承门．　[21]西单．　[22]平则门．　[23]阜成门．　[24]西直门．　[25]肃清门．　[26]健德门．　[27]德胜门小关．　[28]安贞门．　[29]安定门小关．　[30]南河沿．　[31]北河沿．　[32]西皇城根．　[33]地安门．　[34]灵星门．　[35]午门．　[36]太和殿．　[37]景山公园．　[38]煤山．　[39]隆福宫．　[40]兴圣宫．　[41]太液池．　[42]万宁桥．　[43]中心阁．　[44]大天寿万宁寺．　[45]钟楼．　[46]高粱河．　[47]通惠河．　[48]海子．　[49]金水河．　[50]西四．　[51]刘三．　[52]致和．　[53]后英房．　[54]嫦娥．　[55]旧鼓楼大街．　[56]至正．　[57]元顺帝．　[58]洪武．

Lan Hsin-wen

Finds from Kansu

*D*URING the Cultural Revolution a great number of ancient relics have been discovered in Kansu Province, some of them being important finds of primitive culture.

In September 1967, 340 bronze pieces, dating back to the early period of the Western Chou Dynasty (about 11th century-770 B.C.), were brought to light at Paitsaopo, Lingtai County. Finely made and plain in style they were intact and well preserved with the cast inscriptions still clearly visible. There was also a jade chisel carved in the image of a slave.

In 1967, 17 bronzes of the Chin Dynasty[1] (221-207 B.C.) were excavated at Shangyuanchia, Chinan County. Of these, a bronze weight is inscribed with the imperial mandates of the First and Second Emperors, reflecting the unification of China by Chin and the establishment of a centralized government. The other objects, while similar to those of the Warring States Period, have a style of their own, a style which developed later in Han Dynasty vessels. Of particular interest is a novel bronze lamp which

31

becomes three lamps at the turn of a rotary pivot at the edge. Covered with a lid it becomes portable. The lamp illustrates a high artistic skill.

A rich "underground museum," an Eastern Han Dynasty (A.D. 25-220) tomb, was found in 1969 at Leitai, Wuwei County. It contained 220 pieces of lacquerware, gold, bronze, iron, jade, bone and stone articles, including 14 bronze chariots, 17 bronze horses with riders and 45 bronze figurines of chariot driv-

Bronze weight, Chin Dynasty, unearthed in Kansu in 1967.

ers, chariot escorts, male and female servants. A masterpiece of nearly 2,000 years is a unique, lively horse of bronze, galloping and neighing with its head and tail high. To show its speed the unknown craftsman, with a bold imagination, placed its right hind hoof on a flying swallow, and the other three hoofs in the air. The craftsmanship is extremely fine and conforms to the principles of mechanics.

Relics of primitive culture were also discovered in Kansu. A container lid in the shape of a mask, excavated in 1967 at Tsaichiaping, Tienshui County, is a typical relic of Yangshao Culture[2] of the late neolithic period 6,000

32

Bronze galloping horse, Eastern Han Dynasty, unearthed in Leitai, Wuwei County, Kansu Province.

Painted pottery jug dated 5,000 years ago, unearthed in Lanchow in 1966.

years ago. Made of hard red clay, it is a fine example of the level attained in sculpture at that time. Painted pottery jugs, bowls and jars unearthed in September 1966 at Wangpaopaocheng, Lanchow, dating 5,000 years back, are relics of the category of Machiayao Culture.[3] Made of fine hard clay and brightly painted, these vessels are well shaped and fired. They are decorated with symmetrical designs of concentric circles and waves composed mainly of black lines. Copper and painted pottery pieces found at Huangniangniangtai, Wuwei County, are relics of the 4,000-year-old Ch'ichia Culture.[4] They show that Ch'ichia Culture was contemporary with Lungshan Culture[5] of the Yellow River valley, both being of the chalcolithic period. At Mapaochuan, Tienshui County, and at Szeping, Weiyuan County, the stratigraphic correlation between Ch'ichia and Yangshao Cultures was found, which proves

33

that Ch'ichia Culture came later than Yangshao Culture, thus disproving bourgeois scholars who claimed otherwise.

These new archaeological finds of primitive culture testify to the thesis of Chinese archaeologists that Kan-su's primitive culture was the same as that of the middle reaches of the Yellow River.

---

[1] 秦. [2] 仰韶文化. [3] 马家窑文化. [4] 齐家文化. [5] 龙山文化.

Ch'u Tomb and Weapons from Changsha

C HANGSHA, Hunan Province, was an important city on the southern border of the State of Ch'u[1] during the Spring and Autumn and the Warring States Periods[2] (about 770-221 B.C.). The Ch'u tombs have been known for a long time. In 1971, a new Ch'u tomb was opened at Liuchengchiao, Changsha, adding to the already large collection of Ch'u relics.

The Liuchengchiao tomb was discovered in February 1971 by citizens of Changsha's East District and unearthed by Hunan's archaeologists with the co-operation of the local Party and government institutions and people.

The tomb, 6 by 4 m., contained a nest of three coffins, which were 7 m. below ground. Since the whole structure was sealed with a 60-cm. layer of preservative white clay, the coffins, bamboo and wooden articles and silk fabrics were found intact and well preserved. The walls of the outer coffin were made of square cypress blocks 34 cm. on a side, precisely and compactly fixed with bronze nails in a jig-saw pattern. The intermediate coffin consisted of wooden boards 8 cm. thick, dovetailed by tenons and fastened with bronze nails. The inner coffin, 2.17 m. long, 0.82 m. wide and 0.94 m. high, is painted black outside and red inside. The coffin lid and sides are made of three whole crescent-shaped boards, forming an arc seldom seen in Ch'u tombs previously opened. The coffins reveal a high carpentry skill.

The 270 funeral objects include pottery, bronze, jade and bamboo articles, lacquerware, silk fabrics, fruit seeds and pebbles. Of the pottery, there are cooking pots (one with cord pattern), food containers, wine vessels, platters, basins and water jars. The bronzes consist mainly of weapons such as swords, ko^3 (dagger-axe), mao^4 (spear), chi^5 (halberd) and arrow heads, harness pieces such as bar bits and chariot trappings (chiefly chariot decorations like projecting hubs). The lacquerware includes chariot canopies, se^6 (a 23-string-ed zither), hand drums and finely engraved lacquered wood gargoyles (placed at the entrances to rulers' tombs to ward off evil spirits), lacquered tables, wooden platters and lively lacquered wooden deer

Pottery pot with cord pattern.

36

prostrate with their heads coiled. Among the bamboo articles are bows, and mattresses and baskets of novel design. The silk fabrics are of regular and close weave, with 42 warp and 32 weft threads per centimetre.

The funeral objects of the Liuchengchiao tomb predate the Ch'u tombs of the Warring States Period previously found at Changsha. Both in shape and decoration its pottery vessels were modelled after those of the Spring and Autumn Period bronzes. The lacquer objects are also similar to those of the Spring and Autumn Period Ch'u tombs found at Chiangling in Hupeh Province and at Hsinyang in Honan Province. The lacquered winged cups, wooden figurines and bronze mirrors commonly seen in the Ch'u tombs of the Warring States Period are lacking. Nor are the wooden coffins similar. This shows that the Liuchengchiao tomb dates back to the late Spring and Autumn Period, about the 5th century B.C.

The huge outer coffins, the rich and exquisite funeral objects, particularly the variety of weapons, indicate that the tomb belonged to an army commander or a general of the southern garrison.

Class contradictions and class struggle grew increasingly acute in the Spring and Autumn and the Warring States Periods. Feudal princes of the various principalities waged continual wars against each other to consolidate and expand their domains and intensify their exploitation and oppression of the working people. An ancient Chinese saying, "There was no just war in the Spring and Autumn Period," reveals the nature of the wars at that time. The large collection of weapons found in the Liuchengchiao tomb — 93 pieces in all, or more than one-third of the funeral objects — testifies to the ruthless wars among the ruling classes. The following is a brief description of some of the weapons:

1. *Ko*, *Mao* and *Chi* of Varying Lengths

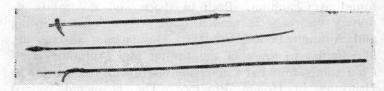

Weapons found intact: *ko* (upper),
mao (middle) and *chi* (lower).

Ko had been a principal weapon since the Shang[7] and Chou dynasties. The inner blade was used to hook or hack, the outer one to attack or thrust and the sharp point to pierce. The *ko* shafts vary in length from 91 cm. to 314 cm.

Mao, also a chief weapon in the Spring and Autumn and the Warring States Periods, with its pointed tip was used for lunging. One of the *mao* has a 280-cm. rattan shaft, the first such *mao* found, the previously discovered ones having wooden shafts. Another *mao* is fitted with a wooden shaft 297 cm. long, whereas those previously found in the Ch'u tombs at Changsha ranged from 165 cm. to 222 cm. in length.

Chi, a combination of *ko* and *mao*, was a fairly advanced weapon in the Spring and Autumn and the Warring States Periods, being used both to hook and hack and to pierce and lunge. On a bronze basin discovered in a tomb at Chihsien County, Honan Province, is shown a battle scene on land and water, in which the *chi* vary in length from half the height of a man to double his height. The iron and wooden *chi* found before at Hengyang and Changsha were 170 cm. and 145 cm. respectively, or the height of a man, while the bronze *chi* unearthed in the Liuchengchiao tomb measure up to 310 cm.

The *ko*, *mao* and *chi* all varied in length for different usages in ancient China. History records that long weapons were used in chariot warfare, while shorter weapons were probably used by foot soldiers.

2. *Shu* — a Weapon in Chariot Warfare

Shu[8] is a pointed but edgeless weapon of *chichu*[9] (substance made of agglutinated sliced bamboo skin), generally 277.8 cm. long according to historical data. Among the Liuchengchiao finds are two pointed but edgeless *chichu* shafts, one 303 cm. and the other 310 cm. They are probably *shu*. *Shu* and the above-mentioned *ko*, long-shaft *chi*, short-shaft *mao* and long-shaft *mao* were the "five weapons in chariot warfare" as historical records put it, planted on both sides of the war chariots. As the Liuchengchiao finds include these five weapons as well as chariot trappings, canopies and horse bits, they are probably a set of chariot warfare equipment.

3. Bows and Arrows

The Liuchengchiao tomb contains 46 arrows, 6 of which are still in good condition. The shafts are 75.7 cm., and the feather tips 14.5 cm. There are three kinds of arrow-heads:

Arrow-heads in three shapes.

(1) prismatic arrow-heads, with a small head, long stem, three barbs and four tips, the frontal tip unusually sharp; (2) flat, leaf-like arrow-heads, with rhombic sections, a pointed frontal tip and two sharp edges; (3) three-winged arrow-heads, with sharp protruding edges and fairly long stems. These vary in form probably for the three purposes as recorded in ancient documents: long distance shooting, short distance shooting (for hunting) and depth shooting (for piercing leather armour). The Liuchengchiao finds also include many bamboo bows of different sizes.

4. Quivers

According to historical records fish-skin and wooden quivers were used in ancient China. According to the bamboo books (made of bamboo strips bound together), previously unearthed from the Ch'u tombs at Changsha, leather ones were also used. A wooden quiver was found at Changsha in 1954. Those discovered in the Liuchengchiao tomb are cylindrical, and made of two 81-cm. crescent-shaped bamboo slabs, the top and the base being roughly the same size. Decorated with fine lacquered geometric designs, they contained still well-preserved arrows.

Study of the weapons from the Liuchengchiao tomb shows that a great change in weapons took place following the progress of society in the Spring and Autumn and the Warring States Periods. While demonstrating the wisdom and creative ability of ancient China's working people, the change also indicates the endless wars the feudal rulers waged against each other to the detriment and misery of the common people.

---

[1]楚国. [2]春秋战国时期. [3]戈. [4]矛. [5]戟. [6]瑟. [7]商. [8]殳. [9]积竹.

41

Chung Chien

Perfect Preservation After 2,100 Years

A 2,100-year-old tomb dating from the Western Han Dynasty (206 B.C.-A.D. 24) was recently discovered on the eastern outskirts of Changsha, Hunan Province, by Chinese archaeologists and excavated with the help of the local people. The corpse, coffin and funeral furniture were all marvelously well preserved. The new discovery has been given the name Han tomb No. 1 at Mawangtui,[1] Changsha.

Well-Preserved Tomb and Body

The city of Changsha has a history of 3,000 years. Metallurgy, textile crafts and lacquer work flourished there as early as the Spring and Autumn and Warring States Periods (770-221 B.C.). During the Western Han Dynasty, when the city was the capital of the local ruler, Prince of Changsha,[2] its economy further advanced.

The newly-excavated tomb is about four kilometres from the city, where the terrain is low rolling hills. The only sign of the tombs that could be seen above ground

Relics from the Han tomb at Mawangtui, Changsha

Colour painting on silk (funeral banner covering the inner coffin).

Details of the painting on sil
Upper: the central section.
Upper right: the upper section.
Lower right: the lower section.

The outer, middle and inner coffins.

The lacquered colour designs on the outer coffin.

Upper: Silk with velvet motif (border of lid and sides of the inner coffin).

Lower: Satin with design of applied coloured feathers (on lid and sides of the inner coffin).

The lacquered colour designs on the middle coffin.

Three-colour embroidery on plain ground.

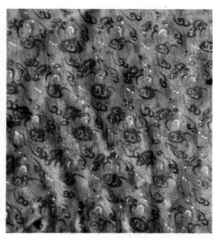

Painted brocade with cloud design.

Polychrome embroidery on orange silk.

Chain-stitch swirls on gauze with lozenge design.

Upper : Gown of plain silk gauze.

Lower : Floss-padded gown in coloured silk painted with gold and silver dust.

Embroidered mittens.

Lacquer tripod.

Lacquer tray with cups and plates.

Lacquer ladles.

Lacquer box and
contained lacquer
red cups.

Set of 12 pitch-pipes and their embroidered case.

Yu pipe.

Wooden se zither.

Musician figurines.

Clothed figurine.

Painted figurines.

View of Mawangtui, Changsha.

were two earthen mounds of similar size and height, standing side by side close together. Han tomb No. 1 is under
the mound to the east. This mound, overgrown with
weeds and brush, stood more than 20 metres high, with a
diameter of 50 metres at the bottom and over 20 metres
at the flat, round top. The lower 7 or 8 metres of the mound
is of local earth; the rest is of earth brought from other
places and rammed down.

The tomb is a vertical rectangular earthen pit approach-
ed through a sloping passageway on the north. It is a
big, well-preserved chamber 16 metres underground. The
chamber is surrounded on all sides by a 30 to 40-cm.-thick
jacket of charcoal weighing altogether 5,000 kg. This layer
of charcoal is itself surrounded and sealed by a layer of

43

sticky and compact white clay. The rest of the pit is filled with mottled reddish clay and sandy yellow earth. Archaeologists are of the opinion that the principal reason for the well-preserved state of the corpse, burial chamber and the quantities of funeral objects is this sealing with charcoal and white clay, which kept out moisture and prevented decay. Suitable soil, temperature and humidity are also factors.

At the bottom of the tomb was a wooden sepulchral chamber built of three layers of planks and resting on three logs at the base of the pit. Inside this wooden chamber were the outer, middle and inner coffins, one inside the other. Except for the space between the outer and middle walls of the wooden chamber, where funeral objects were stored, the other walls, roofs and floors of the wooden chamber as well as the coffins fit one inside the other with practically no space between. All the joining is by the mortise and tenon method.

The lacquered outer and middle coffins are decorated with lively designs in brilliant colours. The wall of the outer coffin, painted in black, bears cloud patterns in white, red, black and yellow, done in flowing lines to give the impression of floating clouds. Among the clouds are monsters grappling with each other, hunting, playing the *se*[3] zither and dancing, or in pursuit of flying birds, fierce beasts, oxen and deer.

The wall of the middle coffin is painted in vermilion. The lid is decorated with cloud patterns in colour and a design of a battle between two dragons and two tigers. The four sides are decorated with designs of mountain peaks,

The outer coffin.

clouds, frolicking dragons, running deer, monsters and *pi*[4] discs enclosed within 11-cm.-wide borders filled with a geometric pattern. These lines are more forceful than those of the art work on the outer coffin.

The lid and sides of the inner coffin are covered with silk decorated with lozenge patterns made with coloured feathers, enclosed within borders embroidered in satin stitch. This is the first time a wooden coffin has been found decorated with such silk.

In the coffin was the corpse of a woman of about 50 years old, wrapped in more than 20 layers of silk and linen, the outer layer bound with nine bands of silk ribbons. The

45

154.5-cm.-long body was laid straight and face up, head to the north. It was so perfectly preserved that there was no sign of deterioration. Doctors from the Hunan Medical College found that the loose connective tissue underneath the skin was still soft and the tissue fibres could be seen clearly. The colour of the femoral arteries was about the same as that in those of the newly dead. When the body was injected with a preservant fluid, there was swelling which later gradually subsided. Two calcified tubercular nodules about the size of peas were found on the hilum and upper part of the left lung.

The unearthed coffins and funeral objects.

The funeral objects bear the inscriptions "Family of the Marquis of Tai"[5] or "Manager of the Household of the Marquis of Tai."[6]   Research based on the inscriptions led to the conclusion that the deceased was the wife of one of the three generations who bore the title Marquis of Tai between 193-141 B.C.

Silks and Paintings

China began sericulture and silk weaving more than 3,000 years ago and as early as the 3rd century B.C. was called Seres, the "Land of Silk."

Large quantities of silk garments and goods, their colours still fresh, were found in the tomb.   There were about 50 pieces of clothing, including stockings, shoes and gloves, over 50 pieces of silk fabrics, some with both borders

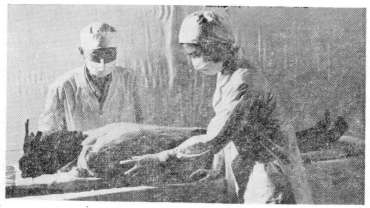

Doctors examining the corpse.

still preserved, and about 20 other pieces of silk for various uses. There were plain silks, gauzes and brocades coloured or decorated in brown, dark brown, yellow-brown, pale yellow, grey, dark red, vermilion, blue-green and white. The animal, cloud, modified cloud, flower and lozenge designs were embroidered, woven or painted on with gold and silver dust. Some gauze pieces are as light as today's nylon netting. One garment of plain silk, the body 128 cm. long and sleeves 190 cm. long, weighs only 49 grammes. Another piece of silk material, 49 cm. wide and 45 cm. long, weighs 2.8 grammes.

Most valuable of all is the painting in colour on a piece of silk draped over the inner coffin. It measures 205 cm. long with the upper part 92 cm. wide and the longer lower part 47.7 cm. wide. Tassels hang from the four lower corners. Beginning from the bottom, the painting shows scenes of the nether world, then of human society and finally of the heavenly world. Some scenes are taken from legends, others from the life of the class society of the time. The painting is executed in flat style, the figures outlined with a single flowing line and filled in with mineral pigments of vermilion, azurite and malachite. The tight composition, brilliantly-contrasting colours and figures exhibiting great liveliness make this a unique work of art. Specialist opinion has hailed it as an important discovery in the history of Chinese art, a valuable addition to the existing paintings from the Western Han Dynasty.

Lacquer and Pottery

The more than 180 pieces of beautiful lacquerware have retained their original glowing colours. They include eared cups, dishes, tripods, vases, square vases, boxes, trays, basins, ewers, handled cups, ladles, round toilet boxes, benches and screens. Of most exquisite design are the eared cups and round toilet boxes. Most of the pieces are of lacquer over a wood base, red on the inside and black on the outside. The designs in black, red and vermilion include stylized leaves, flower petals, clouds and animals as well as geometric patterns. A few are incised with lines as fine as silk thread. The widely-varied and intricately-entwined lines reveal a richly creative mind. Many of the lacquer pieces bear inscriptions in vermilion, red or black lacquer indicating the owner ("Family of the Marquis of Tai"), the use of the object ("For the service of the lord"[7]) or the capacity of the container. In some of the lacquer vessels were found remnants of food — slices of lotus root, chicken bones, fish and products made of rice and wheat.

There are 50 pieces of pottery of a dozen types. They are either clayey grey pottery or hard ware, fired at rather high temperatures. The grey pottery is decorated either with leaf or cloud patterns in colour or with tin foil. The hard ware has a yellow glaze decorated with the impressions of mats or squares. Most of the pottery vessels contained food such as pickled vegetables, fruit (peaches, arbutus, melons), aromatic herbs, bean preserves and dried ginger. The mouths of the hard pottery jars were closed with mud and the impression of a seal with the characters "Manager of the Household of the Marquis of Tai."

Instruments and Other Finds

The three musical instruments among the funeral objects are rare finds. One is a 116-cm. wooden *se* zither, its two ends painted with black lacquer, its frets, four tuning pegs and 25 strings in good condition. It was found in a brocade bag. Another is the 80-cm. *yu*[8] pipes, composed of two rows of reed pipes, 11 in each row. It was also found in a brocade bag and was placed on top of the *se* zither. The third is a set of 12 pitch-pipes made of bamboo of varying lengths and arranged in an embroidered case. The pitch is marked at the bottom of each pipe in black ink.

The 162 wooden tomb figurines are of two sizes. Of the smaller ones, three wear garments of silk or linen; the rest are carved from the split halves of small tree branches, with eyes and eyebrows painted in with ink. Of the bigger figures, some wear real clothes; the clothing for others is indicated in the carving and painted in colour. There are slight differences in the dress, ornaments and hair styles.

Most notable is a set of figurines representing a banquet scene, 18 wearing real clothes, 8 painted in colour. Three are in a standing posture, obviously attendants; the rest are members of a song-and-dance ensemble, some with musical instruments. Found opposite this group were lacquer benches, screens, walking sticks, embroidered pillows, scent bags, toilet boxes and lacquer trays filled with food.

Another valuable find is a set of 312 bamboo slips with writing on them. Their inner side is deep yellow and the back green, as they were made by splitting slender bamboo. Judging from the string marks, the slips were strung together with fine hemp cords at both the top and bottom. The characters are in black ink in the neat *li* or "square plain" style of writing. Most of them can still be made out, showing the slips to be a detailed list of the funeral furniture, including the names, sizes and numbers of the objects. A check showed the list to be fairly accurate.

Other furniture includes 48 bamboo boxes containing clothing and fabrics, straw mats, medicinal herbs, foodstuffs, vegetables, grain seed, seals and several hundred pieces of money of unbaked clay with clear inscriptions. The boxes were sealed with clay impressed with the imprint of the seal, "Manager of the Household of the Marquis of Tai."

BOTH the construction of the tomb and the funerary deposits reflect the economic level of the Western Han period. They are valuable materials for the study of China's textile crafts, lacquer work, painting, music, and customs in clothing and ornaments of that period.

The Marquis of Tai was just one of many minor aristocrats and enjoyed the revenue of a territory with only 700 households. But from the tremendous amount of money and labour that went into the "comforts" for a dead member of the ruling class — as indicated by the finds in this tomb — one can well imagine the waste and extravagance pursued by the living of those days, and their ruthless oppression of the working people. Finds such as in this tomb will enable us to learn more about the class struggle in ancient China.

---

[1]马王堆． [2]长沙王． [3]瑟． [4]璧． [5]"轪侯家"． [6]"轪侯家丞"． [7]"君幸食"． [8]竽．

Hsia Nai

More Finds Along the Silk Road

*C*HINA was the first country in the world to raise silk-
worms and weave fabrics of silk.   More than 3,000
years ago, the people of the late Shang Dynasty were already
engaged in sericulture.   They produced multi-coloured em-
broideries and beautiful damask-like silks (later referred
to as damask)[1] in plain weave with patterns in twill weave.
Later on, fine silk gauzes and polychromes appeared.

In the Han Dynasty (206 B.C.-A.D. 220), China's
technique in silk weaving was further developed.   Among
the Han fabrics were white silk translucent as ice, silk gauze
light as a cloud and damask whose name has become a
synonym for beauty.   To this day the Chinese people have
always compared the beauty of their motherland to brocade
and embroidery.

The silks of the Han Dynasty evoked astonishment
and admiration in central and western Asia and in Europe.
The ruling class of the Roman Empire grudged nothing
to pay for silks from China.   According to a Roman writer,
Chinese silks sold in the city of Rome for their weight in
gold.   Of China, a third-century Roman monk wrote,

"The Seres make precious figured garments bright like flowers and fine as a spider's web." The Chinese were called the Seres — the silk people — and later the trans-Asian route for the silk trade became known as the Road of the Seres, the Silk Road.[2]

THE Silk Road started from Changan, capital of the Western Han Dynasty (206 B.C.-A.D. 24), and passed through the Kansu Corridor and the oases north and south of the Tarim Basin in Sinkiang. It crossed the Pamirs, then traversed central and western Asia straight to the east coast of the Mediterranean. Its total length was 7,000 km., the longest major trade route in ancient times. West of the Pamirs one route went through Ferghana and Samarkand (now both in the Uzbek Soviet Socialist Republic) to Merv[3] (now in the Turkmen Soviet Socialist Republic). Another route passed Balkh in Afghanistan to Merv. From there it continued westward through Hecatompylos, now Damghan in Iran, capital of ancient Parthia,[4] and Ecbatana, now Hamadan, to Ctesiphon-Selencia,[5] near the present Baghdad, on the Tigris. Then it ran through Palmyra in Syria to ports on the east coast of the Mediterranean, Antioch in Turkey or Tyre in Lebanon. It was here that the goods were taken by sea to Alexandria in Egypt or to the Italian peninsula.

Of course merchandise other than silk was transported along this route, such as rhubarb and cinnamon bark from China, and, going eastwards, woolen fabrics from central and western Asia and Roman glassware. But the main cargo was silk.

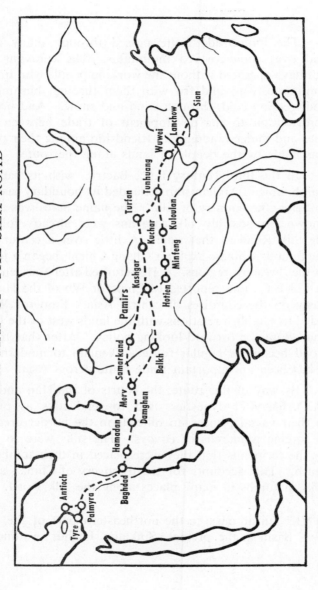

SKETCH MAP OF THE SILK ROAD

The long trade route passed through many deserts and over snow-covered mountains. The caravans could not have operated without the working people who travelled continuously to and fro with them through burning heat and freezing cold, through wind and snow. And no small contribution to the development of trade between countries and understanding and friendship among their peoples was made by the people of lands along the route.

In the third century B.C., Bactria, with its capital at Balkh, now in Afghanistan, extended its boundary eastwards to Seres, the country of silk. The name Seres was already known, so possibly silk caravans were already following the Silk Road at that time. A little over a century later the famous Chinese explorer Chang Chien[6] began a journey to the "western regions."[7] He returned after thirteen years, in 123 B.C., and reported to Emperor Wu of the Han Dynasty on the countries of central Asia. Emperor Wu decided to establish relations with the lands west of the Pamirs and adopted a forward-looking policy. After that the Silk Road became a regular route. Even up to modern times it has been an important trade route across Asia.

By way of this route, the courts of the Han and Tang (A.D. 618-907) dynasties used to send silks as presents to their vassal princes, to officials in the border areas and to foreign monarchs or envoys. The silks were so prized by the recipients that they were placed in their tombs after death. This accounts for the discovery of China's ancient silks in tombs in many places along the Silk Road.

THE Turfan oasis in the northeastern part of the Tarim Basin in the present Sinkiang Uighur Autonomous

Region was a major stopover on the Silk Road. An important discovery was made there at Astana near the county town of Turfan during the Cultural Revolution. In a burial ground dating from the fifth to the eighth centuries where much ancient silk had been found earlier, over a hundred tombs with a great quantity of ancient silk were unearthed.

Among the finds was a pair of silk polychrome shoes from the Eastern Tsin Dynasty (A.D. 317-420). The colours have remained bright through more than 15 centuries. Against a white background is an all-over pattern in red, blue and several other colours, framing the Chinese characters for "good luck." This pattern and the characters were a tradition from the Han Dynasty. Silk shoes in the same style had been found earlier in Han tombs near Lop Nor, south of Turfan.

Two other pieces of silk polychrome in the traditional Han warp-patterned weave have been found in tombs dated A.D. 567 and 631. But in these the cloud scrolls and Taoist mountains characteristic of Han silks are no longer present, being replaced by more

Silk fabrics of the Tang Dynasty (618-907) found in Turfan, Sinkiang.

naturalistic portrayals. In the first piece, several animals interlinked in a horizontal arrangement retain some of the style of the Han cloud-scroll motif. In the second piece, each animal — a bull, a lion and an elephant with rider — is a separate element of design. This may be regarded as a deterioration of the brisk, lively animal designs of the Han Dynasty.

In most of the recent finds of Tang polychromes the pattern is created in the weft, a new method of weaving at that time. They are in typical Tang designs of two main types — clusters of flowers or birds and flowers, or pairs of birds, beasts or riders enclosed by rings of "pearls," that is, small white dots.

The most magnificent of the first type is a polychrome found in a tomb dated A.D. 778. Against a dark red background are flying phoenixes amid red flowers and green leaves. The wefts for each pattern unit are in five shades, blue, orange, white, red and green. It belongs to a comparatively later period and is most representative of the new level of polychrome weaving achieved in the Tang Dynasty.

The second kind of design shows the marked influence of the Sassanian (Persian) silks. In fact, the weft-patterned weave was the traditional method used in the regions of Persia and Syria. The Chinese weavers adopted it and with it partly replaced the warp-patterned weave of the Han Dynasty, a good example of East and West learning from each other through cultural intercourse. Birds and animals form the main motifs — peacocks, ducks, cocks, deer, boar's heads and sometimes riders, often in a symmetrical arrangement and encircled with "pearls," a characteristic Sassanian design.

DAMASK, known since the late Shang Period, had developed into a fabric of very fine quality by the time of the Han Dynasty. It was generally made with a linked-lozenge pattern, sometimes with figures of birds or beasts facing each other inside the lozenges. One of the recent finds is a delicately patterned piece of purple damask dated A.D. 604. In this piece the lozenge shape had evolved into linked ellipses formed by double lines. There are spirals between the lines and small lozenges and flowers between the ellipses. Inside them are the characters meaning "honour."

Silks with dyed designs were a new variety which appeared after the Han Dynasty. They were produced either by the tie-and-dye method or by wax-resist dyeing. In the first, before dyeing, the fabric was tied or gathered with thread into tight bunches which the dye did not penetrate. When the thread was taken out after dyeing, a flowered pattern became visible. The second is the method known as batik — painting a design on the fabric with hot liquid wax which resists the dye. Not only simple flower motifs were produced by this method but complicated ones of floral sprays, birds and deer.

New examples of both kinds of dyed silk have been recently found. On one piece the gathering had not been taken out, revealing how the tie-and-dye method was used. A batik piece had a pattern of mandarin ducks facing each other under a flowering plant. Clothes made with these two kinds of dyed silk, especially the tie-and-dye variety, are often seen in wall paintings and pottery figurines dating from the Northern Wei (A.D. 386-534) to the Tang dynasties.

Ancient silk gauze came either plain or with an all-over pattern. Already in the Han Dynasty, patterned silk gauze was made on the drawloom, an advanced type of equipment. Lozenges were a common decorative element. In the Tang Dynasty complicated designs were made by resist dyeing. A piece of recently-found silk gauze in a distinctive style shows a lively hunting scene with riding hunters aiming their arrows at fleeing deer and hares. These and flowers and plants are in light green against a dark green background, indicating that the fabric was probably dyed twice.

BY studying the new finds of ancient silk from Turfan we can see the technical level of China's silk weaving at the time and the high intelligence and skill of ancient China's working people. The fact that these silks are found at a stopover on the Silk Road shows how China's silk spurred prosperity of this trade route and its importance in the history of world culture. It was a thoroughfare not only for trans-Asian trade but for East-West cultural exchange. The new discoveries again show that the deep friendship, cultural intercourse and mutual supply of needs now existing between the Chinese people and the peoples of other countries can be traced back to a very early date.

---

[1]文绮. [2]丝绸之路. [3]木鹿. [4]安息国. [5]泰西封—塞琉西. [6]张骞. [7]"西域".

Lu Wen-kao

Tomb of the Ming Prince of Lu

*T*HE tomb of Chu Tan,[1] Prince of Lu[2] of the Ming
    Dynasty, was opened in 1970.

Chu Tan was the tenth son of Chu Yuan-chang,[3]
first emperor of the Ming Dynasty. He was born in 1370,
the 3rd year of Hung Wu (designation of Chu Yuan-chang's
reign). Made Prince of Lu at the age of two months, he
went to Yenchow[4] in Shantung, seat of his principality,
at the age of 15. He died in the 22nd year of Hung Wu
(1389), when he was only 19, and was buried at the southern
foot of Chiulung Mountain, present-day site of the Shangchai Production Brigade of the Chunghsin People's Commune, Tsouhsien County, Shantung.

Chu Tan's tomb consists of two parts: two chambers
and an underground passage, with an entire length of about
100 metres. The front chamber is perpendicular to the
main one, together measuring over 20 metres. Before
the front chamber extends an underground passage. The
chambers were built of huge bricks deep in the mountain.
Both are guarded by a stone gate lacquered in red. The
gate to the front chamber was blocked first by a "*chinkang*

wall"[5] (wall of guards) 8.2 metres high and then by another wall 3 metres thick, known as the "gate-sealing wall." The floor of the tomb is 26 metres below the ground level, which indicates the magnitude of the whole structure. It is estimated that the work of digging the tomb, building the chambers and ramming earth involved more than 200,000 cubic metres of earth and stone, requiring more than 800,000 workdays.

In the winter of 1969, during the Cultural Revolution when the peasants of the Shangchai Production Brigade were building terraced fields on Chiulung Mountain, they ran into a large mass of rammed earth and promptly reported to the authorities in charge of cultural relics. An on-the-spot investigation confirmed indications in historical records and folklore that the rammed earth was part of the tomb of Chu Tan.

Under the charge of the revolutionary committee of the Shantung Museum a "three-in-one" excavation team was formed of representatives from the P.L.A., people's commune and archaeological workers. Throughout the undertaking they received the support and aid of the revolutionary committees at all levels in the province, and of the local workers and peasants.

At the initial stage of the excavation serious cave-ins of the rammed earth along the underground passage halted the work. Skilled coal miners came many miles bringing equipment, and shored up the passage and enabled the excavators to proceed safely. When the work of pulling down the "gate-sealing wall" was held up by the seepage of underground water from the chamber, technicians from

Archaeological workers and people excavating a Ming tomb at Tsouhsien County, Shantung.

the nearby Anshang Production Brigade arrived promptly and solved the problem with two pumps.

Breaking open the "gate-sealing wall" was difficult because the bricks were huge and cemented layer upon layer. Workers, peasants and P.L.A. men came to help. Soon the red-lacquered gate was in sight. On top of it was a massive stone weight to keep the gate frame steady. But now pressure cracked the frame and it sank, blocking the gate. In order to prevent damage to the lower part of the structure in case the stone fell, two stonemasons suggested splitting the stone and getting rid of it. This work was done and the gate was opened at last.

The entire excavation took six months, from April 1970 till January 1971, exclusive of the rainy season.

Chu Tan's coffin, coffin case and most of the funeral objects had remained in fairly good condition because the underground water had served as a preservative, keeping air out and maintaining a constant, low temperature. About a thousand funeral objects were found including the prince's grand seal and others, his crown, hats, robes, entourage figurines, zither, chessboard and pieces, calligraphy, paintings, writing-brushes, ink-stick and ink-stone, writing-paper, lacquer furniture, fabrics of silk, cotton and hemp and vessels of gold, jade, bronze and porcelain.

The "Treasure of the Prince of Lu" — the grand seal symbolizing his royal power — and the entourage figurines were found in the front chamber. The entourage comprises two carriages in miniature, 380 human and 24 horse figurines. Some of the human figurines carry swords, lances, melon-shaped bludgeons, halberds, battle-axes and other weapons; others hold canopies, fans, etc., and beat drums or blow the *sheng*[6] (a kind of mouth-organ with pipes). There are also courtiers among the figurines. The pompous procession is a symbol of Chu Tan's tyranny over the working people of his time.

Among the other funeral objects from the chambers are:

Over 300 books printed in the Yuan Dynasty (1271-1368). These are new materials useful for research into Chinese cultural heritage and the study of different editions.

Four scrolls of calligraphy and paintings of the Sung[7] and Yuan dynasties. These include a painting of sunflowers on a silk fan, a painting of blossoming hibiscus and butterflies, with an inscription in gold by Chao Kou[8] (1107-1187), the emperor Kao Tsung of the Southern Sung Dynasty,[9] in his own calligraphy. The painting of hibiscus and butterflies, characterized by exquisite and precise brush work, is strikingly vivid and life-like.

A 7-stringed zither, with the maker's name Lei Wei[10] of the Sung Dynasty given in the 2-line inscription beneath the waist of the instrument.

Silk, cotton and hemp fabrics in a variety of designs, square lacquer cases and a lacquer case to hold the royal tablets, both painted with dragons in gold, and a crystal deer-shaped paper-weight in a beautiful artistic style.

The unearthed objects have been handled carefully, being fixed, stripped, mounted, washed or dehydrated, according to need.

The excavation of Chu Tan's tomb and the large quantities of cultural relics unearthed provide important materials for our study of the political, economic and cultural features of the feudal society in which he lived.

---

[1]朱檀. [2]鲁. [3]朱元璋. [4]兖州. [5]金刚墙. [6]笙. [7]宋. [8]赵构. [9]宋高宗. [10]雷威.

Chang Li-chuan and Lin Yu-ching

The Masses Support Archaeological Work

*M*ANY of the numerous cultural relics brought to light during the Cultural Revolution have been contributions by workers, peasants and People's Liberation Army men. Many inspiring stories have been told of their activities in supporting archaeological work.

For the State

In the spring of 1968 people came to an exhibition of new relics arranged by the Wenhsien County (Honan Province) Revolutionary Committee. These included 21 ancient weapons, musical instruments and vessels, all of which had been discovered by the peasants of Hsiaonanchang Village while levelling the fields. The peasants turned them over to the state.

Such donations have occurred many times since the Cultural Revolution. Workers, peasants and armymen have realized more deeply the significance of protecting cultural relics in the light of Chairman Mao's teaching: **"A splendid old culture was created during the long period of Chinese feudal society."** Whenever they have made such discoveries, they send them to the state. They also notify the responsible departments of clues to hidden treasure that have come to their knowledge.

Among the exhibits in the Museum of Chinese History in Peking is a seal with the inscription "Command of Ten Thousand Troops"[1] which belonged to a subordinate of Han Lin-erh,[2] leader of the "Red Turban Army,"[3] a peasant force that rebelled at the end of the Yuan Dynasty (about 1368). It was unearthed and presented in 1969 by two peasants of the Changchuang People's Commune, Tsaochuang City, Shantung Province. A commune member at Hsincheng County, Honan Province, presented two square bronze wine-vessels of 37 catties each, dated in the Spring and Autumn and the Warring States Periods (770-221 B.C.), which he came upon while irrigating the fields. The peasants also donated large quantities of *ying yuan*[4] gold coins (97.5 per cent pure gold) of the State of Ch'u of the Warring States Period which were unearthed in Anhwei Province.

In February 1970 peasants of the Huangtsun People's Commune, Ninghsiang County, Hunan Province, brought to light a loop-handled bronze ewer[5] when they were digging on a mountain slope. The ewer is beautifully shaped, with a delicate and vivid design. Inside were over 300 jade pieces. The peasants sent the ewer and its contents to the Hunan Provincial Museum.

Recent finds in Ninghsiang, Hunan, indicate that 3,000 years ago when King Chou of Yin⁶ was overthrown by the Chou Kingdom, the slave-owner nobles of Yin fled the Central Plain, carrying large quantities of bronzeware and other objects. On their way south some lightened their load by burying the objects. As time went on, the earth was gradually washed away and the objects exposed.

Joining in the Excavation Work

Workers, peasants and P.L.A. men always volunteer to help archaeological workers in excavation. The unearthing of the two Han tombs at Mancheng, Hopei Province, is a typical example. The tombs were discovered by the P.L.A. men stationed there. The excavation team was made of technical personnel from the Institute of Archaeology of the Chinese Academy of Sciences, members of the Archaeological Team of Hopei Province and armymen.

The tombs of Liu Sheng, Prince of Chungshan, and his wife Tou Wan were built during their lifetime and deeply concealed against discovery. After each burial the passage leading to the tomb chamber was blocked with stones and the tomb gate sealed with molten iron into an "iron wall." These "iron walls" and "stone walls" caused considerable trouble for the excavators, but no difficulties could deter the P.L.A. men and the archaeological workers. They succeeded in opening the passage to Tou Wan's tomb by removing the "stone wall" piece by piece and blowing up the "iron wall" with dynamite. Entrance into Liu Sheng's tomb was made through its already exposed roof.

68

The P.L.A. men also worked together with the archaeological workers in uncovering two suits of "jade clothes sewn with gold thread" and thousands of funeral objects from the tombs. Others took part in surveying, drafting and photographing. They were praised by the local people as versatile in fighting, productive labour and now cultural work.

The tomb of Chu Yueh-lien on Fenghuang Mountain, Chengtu, Szechuan Province, was also opened with the help of the P.L.A. men stationed there and people's commune members. Chu, eldest son of Prince of Shu, died in 1409. His tomb is larger than either of the Mancheng tombs. When unearthed in 1970, underground water had seeped in more than knee-deep and commune members came to help with their pumps and planks.

Peking workers were the first to discover the barbican entrance to Ho Yi Men of Tatu, capital of the Yuan Dynasty in the period of 1271-1368, while taking down the old city walls. The wall inside bore inscriptions illegible from weathering; nevertheless, they traced and copied down the words. From the record the gate was identified as the barbican built by the Yuan rulers to resist the rebellious peasant army and later covered by the Ming walls which were being removed.

Such examples of co-operation between archaeological workers and the masses are too many to enumerate, but the following examples are worthy of mention:

Opening of the tomb of Chu Tan, Prince of Lu of the Ming Dynasty, in Shantung;

Opening of some 140 Tang tombs at Turfan, Sinkiang, by the region's museum.

In their participation in the above undertakings the P.L.A. units and people's communes demonstrated a socialist co-operative spirit by supplying manpower and materials whenever needed.

Caring for the Cultural Heritage

Ever since the People's Republic of China was founded in 1949 the Chinese Communist Party and the people's government have taken measures to protect archaeological finds and historical sites. These measures have been supported by cadres, workers, peasants and P.L.A. men and, later, by Red Guards during the Cultural Revolution.

Yin Hsu,[7] well-known site of Yin ruins, situated at present-day Anyang City, Honan Province, was the capital of the Shang (Yin) Dynasty, from King Pan Keng[8] to the last ruler King Chou, for 273 years (14th-11th centuries B.C.). It has remained intact thanks to the co-operation of the people.

Another well-preserved historical site is the Temple to Ssuma Chien (145 or 135 B.C.-?) at Hancheng County, Shensi Province. Ssuma Chien, famous historian and man of letters of the Han Dynasty, wrote the first Chinese general history *Shih Chi* (*Historical Records*). His temple has a wide attraction for visitors. Teng Shih-yu, caretaker of the historical site since 1958, is a former Red Army soldier who was disabled. He said, "I feel it a great honour to be entrusted with this work by the Party. I am determined to prove myself capable of the task."

Shensi Province, where the capital of various dynasties was located, holds an important place in Chinese history and has an enormous wealth of extant cultural legacies. Before liberation, imperialism in collusion with the Kuomintang reactionaries pillaged much of the province's cultural treasure.

During the Cultural Revolution, the leading body of Shensi, guided by Chairman Mao's proletarian revolutionary line and relying on the masses, organized a team, with the poor and lower-middle peasants as core, to protect cultural relics in the province. Specialists were appointed in 36 cities and counties of the province to carry out the plan for archaeological work.

The Pao-Hsieh Path[9] — a trail across Chinling Mountains running hundreds of miles from the southern end of the Pao River valley northward to the end of Hsiehku valley in Meihsien County in central Shensi — was built by the working people 2,000 years ago. It winds through steep mountains at the side of treacherous waters. Path breakers cleared bramble and thistle, cut the trail across the face of cliffs and put up planks for bridges at the most difficult sections. Shih Men[10] (Rocky Gate) is the "neck" of the path, a tunnel 15 metres long, 4 metres wide and 5 metres high. The interior of the tunnel, the cliff faces and even the rocks in the rushing waters are covered with inscriptions and graffiti from the dynasties of Han (206 B.C.-A.D. 220) and Wei[11] (A.D. 220-280). Some of these are of great value in the study of calligraphy and the methods of building roads, bridges and culverts in ancient China.

In 1969 a reservoir was to be constructed in the Hanchung area in southern Shensi. As Shih Men was in the area to be covered by the reservoir, it had to make way and its inscriptions had to be moved.

A team organized for the removal carefully chiselled the inscriptions and graffiti off section by section. Some which could not be removed were duplicated by plastercasting, photographing or stone rubbing. Collective effort sent the inscriptions and graffiti safely to a new place.

Without the active support of the broad masses of the people it would have been inconceivable for China's archaeological workers to achieve the successes in preserving the cultural relics.

---

[1]"管军万户府". [2]韩林儿. [3]红巾军. [4]郢爱. [5]提梁卣. [6]殷纣王.
[7]殷墟. [8]盘庚. [9]褒斜道. [10]石门. [11]魏.

中国新出土文物

＊

外文出版社出版（北京）
1972年（32开）第一版
1973年第二版
1974年第二次印刷
编号：（英）11050—73
00080
11—E—1262PA